Nelson

Spelling

Developing Skills

John Jackman

4

BOOK FOUR

Scottish Adviser: Iain Campbell

CONTENTS/SCOPE AND SEQUENCE

Page	Focus	Extra	Extension	Focus resource	Extension resource
34/35 Unit 14 simple plurals	matching key words to pictures	+s +es +ies	some plural exceptions	writing target plurals	writing target plurals and related rules
36/37 Unit 15 more plurals	matching key words to pictures	f, fe to ves ff to ffs	words ending in o	writing target plurals	writing target plurals and related rules
38/39 Unit 16 mnemonics	pictorial mnemonics	using and creating mnemonics	using and creating mnemonics	small words in longer words	making mnemonics
40/41 Unit 17 prefixes	the double letter issue	'English' prefixes	alphabetical ordering	un dis in im prefixes	antonyms
42/43 Unit 18 suffixes	matching key words to pictures	dropping or retaining a final e	able / ible	dropping a final e	vowel and consonant suffixes
44/45 Unit 19 more suffixes	adding ed to y endings	adding other suffixes to y endings	suffixes and ll words	adding ed to y endings	adding other suffixes to y endings
46/47 Check-up 2	Check-up 2	Check-up 2	Check-up 2	Check-up 2	Check-up 2
48/49 Unit 20 ie ei	revising the rule	the seven sounds of ie/ei	selecting ie or ei	matching target words to pictures	practising the rule
50/51 Unit 21 history and geography words	matching key words to pictures	misspelt target words	matching target words to definitions	identifying missing letters	crossword puzzle
52/53 Unit 22 ent/ence ant/ance	adding correct word endings	matching adjectives and nouns	target letter pattern adverbs	crossword puzzle	identifying missing letters
54/55 Unit 23 unstressed letters	word grid puzzle	unstressed vowels and consonants	syllables in words with unstressed vowels	practising words with unstressed letters	syllables in words with unstressed vowels
56/57 Unit 24 more tricky words	contractions	problem double letters	using a dictionary to correct spellings	matching words and contractions	mini-crossword puzzles
58/59 Unit 25 ICT and netspeak	matching key words to pictures	misspelt target words	internet and email conventions	labelling using target words	computing word origins
60/61 Unit 26 British English or American English?	comparing British and American spellings	French origins	spotting and changing American spellings	matching American and British spellings	American and British English equivalents
62/64 Check-up 3	Check-up 3	Check-up 3	Check-up 3	Check-up 3	Check-up 3

FLASHBACK

 OCUS

A Look at these pictures and clues.
Write the words in your book.

1 to stare angrily

gl_____

2 a flexible strand of metal

w_____

3 a circle's outer edge

c_____

4 a wild Australian dog

d_____

5 the antonym of satisfied

d_____

6 a desert animal with humps

c_____

7 thought transference

t_____

8 someone who steals

th_____

B Write a word that rhymes with each of these words, and has the same spelling pattern.

1 trays   **2** passes   **3** berries   **4** flies

C Write each of these lists of words in alphabetical order.

1 explore   export   expel   expand

2 husky   hurdle   husband   hurricane   hurling

EXTRA

A List four words based on each of these root words.

  1 help **2** view   **3** care

B Write the plural form of each of these words.

  1 piano **2** potato **3** play **4** leaf **5** activity

C Write two sentences for each of these homonyms to show that they can have more than one meaning.

  1 jumper   **2** fan   **3** order

D Write a homophone for each of these words.

  1 bare   **2** there   **3** cereal   **4** fare
  5 haul   **6** key   **7** paws   **8** stationary

E Copy these words. Circle the unstressed vowels.

  1 separate **2** boundary **3** interested **4** generous

EXTENSION

A Write two words that begin with each of these prefixes.

  1 trans   **2** circum   **3** auto

B Write the singular form of each of these verbs.

  1 wash **2** justify **3** jump **4** worry **5** imply

C Copy these words. Then next to each write the syllables.

  1 regrettably **2** impossibility **3** satisfaction

D Do these word sums.

  1 help + ful = **2** happy + ly = **3** silly + ness =
  4 enjoy + ment =   **5** beauty + fully =

E What are the guide words on the page in your own dictionary on which these words appear?

  1 relief **2** issue **3** conscious **4** atmosphere **5** knowledge

sure
ture

It's the **nature** of the bumble-bee
To seek its golden trea**sure**
Of nectar as it's commonly known,
The bee's great source of plea**sure**.

 FOCUS

KEY WORDS

measure
treasure
leisure
displeasure
exposure
nature
future
picture
puncture
texture
mixture
sculpture
fracture
adventure

Copy these sentences. Use a word from the box to fill each gap.

creature	picture	capture	nature

"Look at that little _____ ," said Bob.

"It's a spider," said his teacher. "Will you draw a ____ of it?"

"Look, it's spinning a web to help it _____ a fly," said Bob.

"Isn't it marvellous how _____ works?" said Mr Chaudhri.

"Yes, as long as you're not a fly!", thought Bob.

A Match each of the **ure** words in the list with the root word from which it has been made.

Copy the two lists of words in your book and draw neat lines to join the related words.

The first one is done to help you.

enclose	failure
fail	pleasure
depart	enclosure
moist	pressure
furnish	departure
press	furniture
please	moisture

B Write sentences using three of the **ure** words.

A Look at the words in the box.

> futuristic featuring endurance security
> lecturer torturing pressurised insurance
> agricultural natural picturesque moist

Each word has a related word with a **ure** ending.

Write the words in the box and next to each write the related **ure** word.

The first one is done to help you.

1 futuristic future

B Use four of the **ure** words in sentences to show their meanings.

ph

sphere

photo

autograph

phone

elephant

microphone

geography

FOCUS

KEY WORDS

- graph
- phantom
- pheasant
- phone
- photo
- physical
- alphabet
- dolphin
- elephant
- geography
- microphone
- pamphlet
- prophet
- sphere

A There are ten **ph** words hidden in this puzzle.
Write them in your book.

a	p	h	a	n	t	o	m	b	g	p
k	l	m	l	c	h	g	r	a	p	h
e	l	e	p	h	a	n	t	e	h	e
m	r	p	h	o	n	e	d	f	o	a
t	s	p	a	m	p	h	l	e	t	s
w	x	i	b	o	p	q	n	u	o	a
a	z	v	e	d	o	l	p	h	i	n
j	b	y	t	p	r	o	p	h	e	t

B Write a sentence that uses two of these **ph** words.

E XTRA

In most words **ph** sounds like **f**. In this list of words every **ph** has been written as an **f**, but be careful - sometimes the **f** should be there! Write the words correctly in your book.

1 alfabet 2 telefone 3 before 4 dolfin

5 sfere 6 geografy 7 pamflet 8 difficult

9 profet 10 fotograf 11 triumf 12 fysical

E XTENSION

Most words that start with, or contain, **ph** are words now used in English that came from the Greek language.

Examples: **phone** - *phone* is Greek for *voice* or *sound*

graph - *graphein* is Greek for *writing*

sphere - *sphaira* is Greek for *ball*

photo - *photos* is Greek for *light*

phobia - *phobos* is Greek for *fear*

A Sort the words in the box into the lists according to their Greek root word.

autograph sphere microphone atmosphere
claustrophobia photograph telephone
agoraphobia graph hemisphere paragraph
saxophone telegraph arachnophobia

graph	sphere	phone	photo	phobia

B Choose four of the words and write a definition of each, using what you know about their Greek origins.

C Use a dictionary to help you find words beginning with **ph** that match these clues.

1 a small bottle for liquids
2 extraordinary; outstanding; remarkable
3 the collection of postage stamps
4 a string of words

You might need a dictionary to help you with some of the definitions.

roots

audience primrose autograph aquarium

FOCUS

KEY WORDS

- bicycle
- aquarium
- aerodynamic
- supernatural
- microscope
- audience
- portable
- transfer
- primrose
- autograph
- geology
- prehistoric

Roots are words or parts of words to which prefixes and suffixes can be added to make words from the same word family.

Copy these words. Next to each write a key word which has the same root, prefix or suffix. The first one is done to help you.

1 biped *bicycle* 2 microcosm 3 audition
4 transplant 5 zoology 6 export
7 aquatic 8 automatic 9 superpower
10 aeronaut 11 primate 12 preview

Roots can often provide a clue to the meaning of a word.
A <u>primary</u> school is the <u>first</u> school we attend (not counting nursery!).
The root **prima** comes from Latin and means *first*.

A Match each of these pairs of words with a root word from the box.

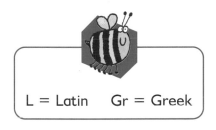

L = Latin   Gr = Greek

aqua (L) water	*scribere* (L) to write	*fluere* (L) to flow
deka (Gr) ten		*duo* (L) two
logos (Gr) word, speech		*ge* (Gr) the earth
metron (Gr) measure		*pedis* (L) a foot

1 *scribble manuscript*   2 *fluid fluent*   3 *duet duologue*
4 *thermometer speedometer*   5 *dialogue monologue*
6 *pedal pedestrian*   7 *aquaduct aquatic*
8 *decade decimal*   9 *geology geography*

B Add another word which has the same root to each pair of words in A.

A Copy these words. Underline the root of each word. Use a dictionary to find the meaning of the words in each group then write what you think each root means.

Be careful!
The root will vary
slightly in some words.

1 *pathetic   sympathy   apathy*
2 *portable   porter   transport*
3 *migrate   immigration   emigrate*
4 *octet   octagon   octopus*
5 *quadruplets   quadrangle   quad-bike*

B Write a word which uses each of these Latin or Greek roots.

1 accidere (Latin for to *happen*)   2 centum (Latin for *hundred*)
3 facere (Latin for to *make*)   4 graphein (Greek for to *write*)
5 monos (Latin for *single*)   6 phone (Greek for *sound*)

11

a
and double letters

A **cann**er exceedingly **cann**y
One morning remarked to his gr**ann**y,
"A **cann**er can can
Anything that he can,
But a **cann**er can't can a can, can he?"

FOCUS

A Match a key word to each of these pictures.

1 all _____

2 att_____

3 ass_____

4 app_____

5 app_____

6 arr_____

B Write sentences using two of these words.

EXTRA

Hidden in the puzzle box are the answers to these riddles.
Write the answers in your book.

a	n	n	i	v	e	r	s	a	r	y
t	a	c	a	t	t	a	c	k	f	z
t	b	a	s	s	i	s	t	a	n	t
e	x	p	s	a	d	w	e	f	z	r
n	q	p	e	l	m	a	c	e	d	l
t	o	e	m	l	a	r	r	e	s	t
i	p	a	b	o	q	z	l	t	v	u
o	w	r	l	w	d	f	y	q	r	l
n	p	z	y	x	e	u	a	b	e	x

1 Take off **ap** and you have a fruit.
2 Drop a **t** and **ion** and you have something for camping.
3 A small pin is in the last part of this word.
4 The front of this word (that ends with **y**) looks like a small horse.
5 The end of this word is the opposite of high.
6 If you're tired you'll like the last four letters of this word.
7 The last three letters are a tiny creature.
8 This happens every year.

EXTENSION

> Remember, a **syllable** is a part of a word that can be said by itself.
> Each syllable has its own vowel sound.
> Like this:
> 'annoy' is pronounced **an / noy**, so it has two syllables.
> 'attention' is pronounced **at / ten / tion**, so it has three syllables.

Does each of your syllables have a vowel sound?

A Copy these words. Sort them into lists of one-syllable, two-syllable and three-syllable words.

1 appear   2 attack   3 all   4 allow
5 assistant   6 assembly   7 annual
8 arranging   9 attempting   10 applaud

1 syllable	2 syllables	3 syllables
add	adding = ad / ding	addition = ad / di / tion

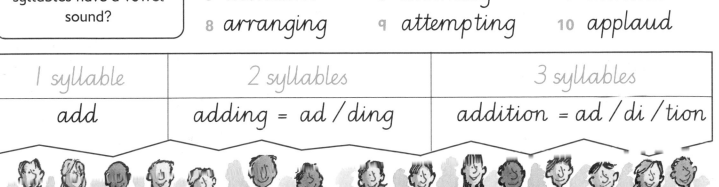

connectives

FOCUS

KEY WORDS

meanwhile
furthermore
therefore
however
nonetheless
alternatively
although
because
nevertheless
whereas
whoever
consequently

A Hidden in the wordsearch box are twelve connectives.
Copy them into your book.

r	g	b	e	a	l	t	h	o	u	g	h
e	m	e	a	n	w	h	i	l	e	l	e
e	o	c	t	d	h	e	s	i	n	c	e
d	r	a	e	q	e	r	v	r	d	f	w
k	e	u	r	s	n	e	w	s	w	s	h
n	o	s	e	r	r	f	p	e	d	t	e
m	v	e	c	w	h	o	e	v	e	r	r
y	e	t	g	h	u	r	u	e	a	e	e
o	r	o	h	o	w	e	v	e	r	y	a
n	e	v	e	r	t	h	e	l	e	s	s

B Copy out the key words that were not in the wordsearch box.

furthermore   then   however   so   nonetheless   but   because therefore   and   moreover   henceforward   whenever   as   with meanwhile   notwithstanding   after   when   although   if since   nevertheless   while   besides   whatever   until   yet   for consequently   whoever   whereas   alternatively

This box contains some of the most frequently used connective words. Copy into your book those that are compound words. Next to each word, write the smaller words that make it. The first one is done to help you.

1 furthermore   further / more

XTENSION

A Copy these sentences, using the words in the box above to suggest words that might be used to fill the gaps.

1 It was an unfair tackle but, _____ , he was determined not to let his pain show.

2 We could meet at 2 o'clock or, _____ , we could meet later back at home.

3 The elderly lady was slow and _____ was nervous of crossing the road alone.

4 He is good at poetry _____ she is better at writing stories.

5 Jahan was looking for the kitten in the house _____ Jade was hunting in the garden.

B Make up three more sentences of your own using some of the connectives you have not used in A and underline the connective you have used.

word origins

kangaroo

cafe

easel

pizza

spaghetti

FOCUS

KEY WORDS

hoist

easel

cafe

restaurant

ballet

shawl

zero

caravan

volcano

pizza

spaghetti

English is a living and changing language. Here are some words borrowed from languages in different parts of the world.

The Netherlands: smuggle easel hoist sketch buoy

France: cafe restaurant boutique ballet banquet beef pork chauffeur

India: verandah bungalow pyjamas shampoo jungle

America: burger toboggan moose blizzard moccasins okay seafood

Australasia: kangaroo boomerang kiwi billabong dingo

A Sort the words into lists according to their area of origin.

The Netherlands	France	India	America	Australasia

B Add some more words to each list if you can.

Onomatopoeia
is the making of words
from the sound they
describe.

The words we use today have come from different sources:

- from other countries   spaghetti (an Italian dish)
- from place names, or people's names   wellingtons (from the boots worn
  by the Duke of Wellington)
- from earlier languages   photograph (*photos* is Greek for
  light)
- from sounds   gurgle   cuckoo

A   Sort these words into lists according to their likely origin.
Use an encyclopedia or a dictionary to help you.

> August   splash   geology   sandwich
> hiss   cardigan   biro   thump   pizza
> autobiography   cello   jangle   sphere
> boomerang   telephone   banquet

From other countries	From names	From old languages	From sounds

B   Try to add two more words of your own to each list.

EXTENSION

These words have come into English from Italian.

> soprano   volcano   pizza   spaghetti   ravioli
> concerto   alto   solo   piano   macaroni
> opera   studio   pasta   confetti   umbrella

A   **1**   Write the words connected with food.
     2   Copy the words connected with music.

B   **1**   Sort the words in the box into lists according to the last letter of
        each one.
     2   What do you notice about the final letter of these Italian words that
        is different from most English words?

Using a dictionary

FOCUS

GIDDY

giddy *adj.* dizzy, light-headed (*comparative* **giddier**, *superlative* **giddiest**). *adv.* **giddily**. *n.* **giddiness**.

gift *n.* 1. a present. 2. a natural ability.
do not look a gift horse in the mouth do not criticize a gift.

gifted *adj.* skilful, clever.

gigantic *adj.* enormous, like a giant. See **giant**.

giggle *v.* to titter, to laugh in an excited way (**giggling, giggled**).

gild *v.* to paint with gold paint.

gill (1) (*pron.* gil) *n.* the breathing organ of a fish or frog.

gill (2) (*pron.* jil) *n.* a liquid measure equal to one-quarter of a pint (0.142 litres)

gilt *n.* a thin layer of gold or gold paint.
to take the gilt off the gingerbread to make something less attractive, from an old custom of gilding gingerbread at fairs.

gin (*pron.* jin) *n.* 1. a trap. 2. an alcoholic drink.

ginger *n.* a tropical root ground to a hot spicy powder for flavouring food.

gingerbread *n.* a biscuit, or bread, flavoured with ginger.

gipsy see **gypsy**.

GLAD

giraffe *n.* a long-necked African animal.

girder *n.* a strong beam holding up a weight.

girdle *n.* a belt, a sash. *v.* **girdle** to surround (**girdling, girdled**).

girl *n.* 1. a female child. 2. a youngish woman. 3. a female servant. *adj.* **girlish** 1. like a girl. 2. belonging to a girl.

girth *n.* 1. a band round a horse holding the saddle in place. 2. the distance round anything.

gist (*pron.* jist) *n.* the main point.

give *v.* 1. to hand over, to deliver. 2. to pay, as *to give a high price*. 3. to yield, as the beam gives under the weight of the roof (**giving, gave, given**).
to give and take to be tolerant.
to give in to surrender.
to give out 1. to let it be known. 2. to run short. 3. to distribute.
to give up to surrender.
to give oneself away to betray oneself.

glacial *adj.* concerning glaciers.

glacier *n.* a slow-moving river of ice.

glad *adj.* pleased (*comparative* **gladder**, *superlative* **gladdest**). *adv.* **gladly**. *v.* **gladden** to please. *n.* **gladness**.

KEY WORDS

letters
words
vowel
consonant
order
alphabet
dictionary
definition
origin
meaning
guide
abbreviation

a b c d e f g h i j k l m n o p q r s t u v w x y z

The words in a dictionary are arranged in alphabetical order. Write each of these lists of words in alphabetical order.

1 horrible dreary commotion orderly stallion

2 microphone magnet metre mystery monsoon

3 lubricate disguise liquorice laundry description

4 holly hobble home horizon honour

5 spruce sprout spring spread sprawl

6 interlude international intersperse interview interrupt

Dictionaries contain lots of information about each word:
- its definition
- what word class (part of speech) it is
  (n = noun; v = verb; adj = adjective)
- its origin, in some cases
- related words or sayings, if it has any.

Use the page from the dictionary on the facing page to help you answer the following questions.

Dictionaries enable us to check the spelling of a word.

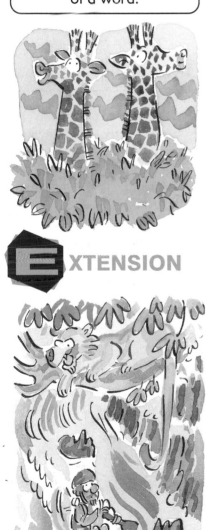

A Write these words, spelling them correctly:

giggal   girarf   glasier   gigantick   gladest

B 1 Which word comes between **gin** and **gingerbread**?
2 Which word follows **girth**?
3 What class of word is **giddy**?
4 What are the comparative and superlative of **glad**?
5 What does **to take the gilt off the gingerbread** mean?
6 What are the two quite different meanings of **gill**?
7 What is the other way to spell **gipsy**?
8 What is the noun related to the adjective **giddy**?
9 What does **to give and take** mean?
10 Which proverb is based on the word **gift**?

EXTENSION

At the top of each page are guide words, which are the first and last word on that page. The guide words on the page opposite are GIDDY and GLAD.

Here are the guide words from three different pages in the dictionary.
IRON – JAR p115   JAUNT – JOUST p116   JOVIAL – KEEP p 117

A Write the number of the page on which the following words would appear?
1 kayak   2 jolly   3 jealous   4 irresistible   5 jacket   6 jubilee
7 keep   8 juror   9 jewellery   10 juice   11 isthmus   12 January

B Use your own dictionary to answer these questions.
What are the guide words on the page on which these words appear?
1 puma   2 slime   3 terminal   4 insult
5 disgrace   6 expectation   7 property   8 squabble
9 congratulate 10 value   11 brigade   12 independence

er
or
ar
endings

What's the most popul**ar** month in the calend**ar**?

FOCUS

KEY WORDS

computer
newspaper
customer
stranger
builder
burglar
calendar
popular
particular
similar
interior
superior
calculator
radiator

---

builder   actor   teacher   miner   doctor
sailor   soldier   driver   conductor   tailor

A Match the words from the box to the pictures below.

1 _____   2 _____   3 _____   4 _____   5 _____

6 _____   7 _____   8 _____   9 _____   10 _____

B Look at the last two letters in your answers in A.
Sort them into two groups.

C Write one sentence that has both a word ending in **er** and a word ending in **or**.

Copy these sentences into your book. Choose a key word to fill each gap.

My parents said they would buy me a _____ to help with my school work. As they are so expensive, we looked for second-hand ones in the _____ .

"Is there a _____ type you want?" asked Dad.

"No, but laptop computers are very _____," I said.

"Yes, it certainly seems a _____ make. There are lots in the paper," said Mum.

"This one looks good," I said. "It has a built-in _____ to give the date, and a _____ to work out all my maths homework for me!"

"I'm not sure about that," replied Mum, "but they are good - it is _____ to the one I use at work."

EXTENSION

A Arrange these groups of words in alphabetical order.

1 instructor   instruct   instruction   instructed   instructing
2 circular   circle   circled   circulation   circling
3 computer   compute   computation   computerise   computed
4 popular   popularise   population   populated   populate
5 calculator   calculation   calculate   calculating   calculated
6 customer   customise   customising   customers   custom

B Without using a dictionary, write a short definition of the first word in each group.

C Now find each of the words from B in a dictionary.
Compare your definition with that in the dictionary.
What other information does the dictionary give about each word?

ory
ary
ery

The **story** of Pirate McTrick**ery**
Is an extraordin**ary** myst**ery**.
He stole by the stash
Jewell**ery** and cash!
Could this be a major discov**ery**?

FOCUS

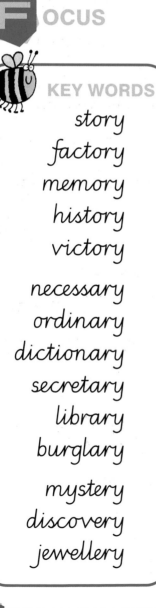

KEY WORDS

story
factory
memory
history
victory

necessary
ordinary
dictionary
secretary
library
burglary

mystery
discovery
jewellery

A Find in the puzzle box three words with each of these endings:

ary   ery   ory

Write them in your book.

b	u	r	g	l	a	r	y	s
m	y	s	t	e	r	y	x	e
v	n	u	r	s	e	r	y	c
i	m	e	m	o	r	y	z	r
c	r	o	c	k	e	r	y	e
t	l	i	b	r	a	r	y	t
o	h	i	s	t	o	r	y	a
r	f	a	c	t	o	r	y	r
y	l	m	e	s	t	o	r	y

B Write and illustrate in your book a fun sentence that uses at least three of the words from the box.

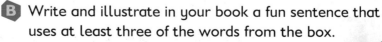

A Finish these words by adding **ory**, **ary** or **ery** to each one. Then use your dictionary and write a meaning for each word you have made.

1 hist＿＿＿　2 necess＿＿＿　3 diction＿＿＿

4 nurs＿＿＿　5 ordin＿＿＿　6 fact＿＿＿

7 machin＿＿＿　8 deliv＿＿＿　9 discov＿＿＿

10 mem＿＿＿　11 burgl＿＿＿　12 tempor＿＿＿

B Copy these words. Next to each one write its root word.
The first one is done to help you.

1 jewellery *jewel*　2 machinery　3 bribery

4 observatory　5 discovery　6 nursery

7 slippery　8 brewery　9 delivery

Notice that the vowel letter in these endings is rather difficult to hear.

C What is the difference in meaning between **stationary** and **stationery**? Work out and write down a way of remembering the difference.

E XTENSION

To make plurals of words ending with **ory**, **ary** or **ery**, remember to change the **y** to **i** before adding **es**, like this:
factory factor**ies**;　library librar**ies**

A Write the plural form of each of these words in your book.

1 secretary　2 memory　3 victory　4 dictionary

5 nursery　6 discovery　7 burglary　8 delivery

9 story　10 brewery

B Write in your book sentences which use the plural forms of these words. You can write fun sentences, but you must use all the words!

1 secretary　burglary　dictionary

2 delivery　brewery　nursery

3 memory　story　victory

unstressed vowels

FOCUS

KEY WORDS

explanatory
memory
secretary
jewellery
poisonous
company
desperate
definitely
difference
voluntary
reference
literature

A Match a key word to each clue.

1 used for personal decoration
2 good books and poems
3 works in an office
4 describes a substance that can kill or harm you
5 anxious with despair
6 describes services given for no reward
7 without doubt
8 a business organisation

B Use three of the words from **A** in a sentence. It can be a fun sentence if you wish.

EXTRA

Remember, **unstressed vowels** are vowel letters which we either do not sound, or do not sound very distinctly, as we speak. Unstressed vowels can cause spelling problems because it is easy to forget them and miss them out.

mem**o**ry

Memory sounds like *memry*, because the **o** is an unstressed vowel.

A Copy these words. Circle the unstressed vowels.

1 necessary   2 boundary   3 ordinary

4 victory   5 factory   6 history

7 mystery   8 slippery   9 machinery

B Use a dictionary to help you spot the unstressed vowels that have been left out of these words. Now write the words correctly.

1 abomnable   2 busness   3 defnitely
4 cathlic   5 categry   6 frightned
7 widning   8 intrest   9 messnger

EXTENSION

It can sometimes help to spell words correctly that have unstressed vowels, if we think of the syllables.

Remember:
- every syllable needs a vowel sound;
- when two consonants separate two vowel sounds, the first syllable usually ends after the first consonant.

hospital   =   hos/pi/tal

This reminds us not to spell the word 'hospitl'.

Copy each of these words into your book, saying them quietly to yourself as you do. Next to each word write out its syllables.

1 separately   2 compromise   3 disinterested

4 preparation   5 memorable   6 stationery

7 abandoned   8 conference   9 unfamiliar

CHECK-UP 1

OCUS

Look at these pictures and clues.
Write the key words in your book.

1 when air leaks from a tyre

p_____

2 modelling in stone

s_____

3 the largest land mammal

e_____

4 an abbreviated form of telephone

p_____

5 place where fish are kept

a_____

6 instrument for measuring temperature

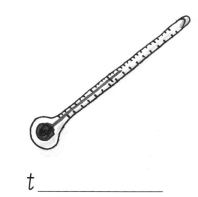

t_____

7 antonym for depart

a_____

8 used for cutting paper

s_____

9 a type of sailing vessel

y_____

10 a thief who breaks into houses

b_____

EXTRA

A Copy and complete these word wheels in your book.

assisting   *transport*

assist   *port*

B Write the small words that make up these connectives.

1 *notwithstanding* 2 *moreover* 3 *whereas*
4 *furthermore* 5 *nonetheless* 6 *however*

C Copy these words and next to each name the country it came from.

1 *spaghetti* 2 *easel* 3 *verandah*
4 *restaurant* 5 *moose* 6 *boomerang*

D What do we call:
1 a person who acts?
2 a person who burgles?
3 a person who makes sick people well?
4 a person who works in an office?
5 a person who works on a building site?
6 precious stones and metals used for personal decoration?

E The unstressed vowels are omitted from these words. Write them in your book correctly.

1 *boundry* 2 *machinry* 3 *intresting*
4 *defnitely* 5 *frightned* 6 *memry*

EXTENSION

A Write two words that have each of these Greek roots.

1 *sphere* 2 *photo* 3 *phone* 4 *graph*

B What are the syllables in each of these words?

1 *acquisition* 2 *circumnavigation*
3 *expiry* 4 *autobiographical*

C Write three music words and three food words which English has borrowed from Italian.

D What are 'guide words' in a dictionary?

tricky words

F OCUS

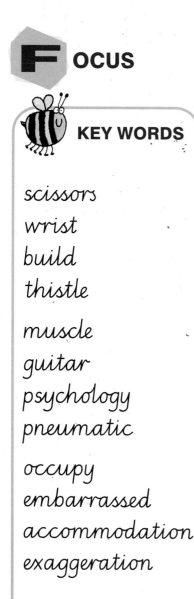

KEY WORDS

scissors
wrist
build
thistle

muscle
guitar
psychology
pneumatic

occupy
embarrassed
accommodation
exaggeration

guard write castle muscle guitar wrong
scent scissors wrist build listen whistle
wreck biscuit scenery thistle

Copy these words neatly into your book. Underline the letters you think someone might forget to put in.

All of these words came into English from the Greek language.
They therefore have some slightly unusual letter patterns.
One letter is omitted from each word. Write them correctly in your book.

1 r_ubarb   2 r_eumatism 3 cata_rh

4 ast_ma   5 paral_se   6 _sychology

7 g_ography   8 g_ometry   9 archa_ology

10 autobiogra_hy 11 micr_scope 12 tel_scope

13 catastroph_   14 apostroph_   15 encyclop_edia

EXTENSION

A Look carefully at these words.
All of the double consonants have been taken out. Think carefully about which should be 'double letters'. Write them correctly in your book.
Use a dictionary to check your final list.

1 exagerate 2 inocent   3 ocupy   4 ocasion

5 paralel   6 posesions 7 sudenes   8 woolen

9 adres   10 vacinate

B A pair of consonants is missing from each gap.
Copy the words adding the missing letters.

1 a__o__odation   a place to live

2 a__ition   adding up

3 a__re__   name of where you live

4 co__i__ee   organized group of people

5 disa__oint   to let someone down

6 di__icult   not easy

7 emba__a__ed   feel awkward

8 qua__el   a disagreement

maths and science words

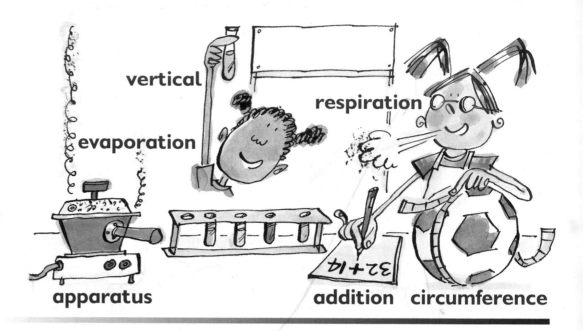

vertical

respiration

evaporation

apparatus

addition circumference

FOCUS

KEY WORDS

addition
subtraction
multiplication
division

parallel
horizontal
vertical
circumference

evaporation
condensation
respiration

apparatus
laboratory

Look at these pictures. Select and write a key word that matches each one.

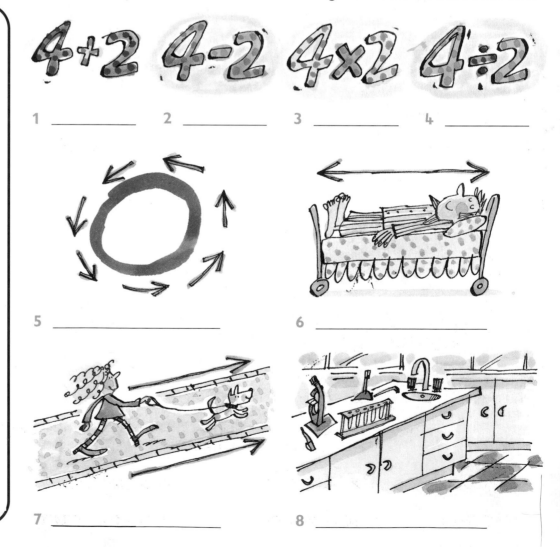

4+2   4-2   4×2   4÷2

1 _____   2 _____   3 _____   4 _____

5 _____   6 _____

7 _____   8 _____

 **XTRA**

All of these maths words are misspelt in a way that often happens. Write them correctly.

When you have finished, check your answers in a dictionary.

1 adition   2 approximatly   3 centimeter

4 curcumfrence   5 horizontle   6 meashure

7 parralel   8 negitive   9 symetrical

10 virtical   11 volumn   12 wieght

XTENSION

A Match a word from the box to each of these definitions.

| mammal evaporate dissolve friction |
| oxygen vertebrate condensation digestion |

1 to turn into vapour

2 one of the gases found in the air, necessary for life

3 an animal with a backbone

4 absorbing food

5 to disappear when stirred in a liquid

6 an object rubbing against another

7 an animal that suckles its young

8 water formed from vapour

B Copy each of these words in turn, writing next to each a simple definition. Use a dictionary to help you.

1 predator   2 perimeter   3 perpendicular   4 rhombus

5 isosceles   6 laboratory   7 parallelogram   8 respiration

homophones

He **threw** the ball and it went **through**.

FOCUS

KEY WORDS

break

brake

threw

through

source

sauce

site

sight

allowed

aloud

waist

waste

peace

piece

A Look at these picture clues.
Write a matching key word for each in your book.

1 _____

2 _____

3 _____

4 _____

5 _____

6 _____

B Write a sentence to demonstrate the meaning of each of the
homophones which match the answers to the six questions in **A**.

EXTRA

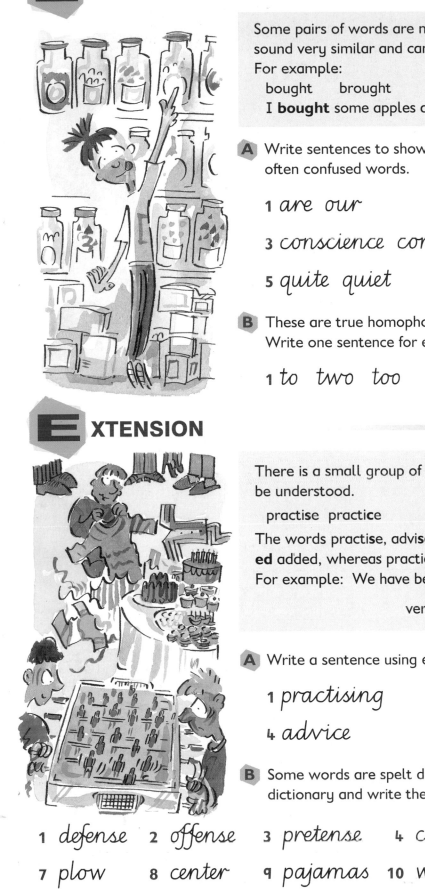

Some pairs of words are not actually homophones although they sound very similar and can cause confusion.
For example:
bought   brought
I **bought** some apples at the shop.   I **brought** them home with me.

A Write sentences to show that you know the difference between these often confused words.

1 are our   2 cloths clothes

3 conscience conscious   4 choose chose

5 quite quiet   6 lose loose

B These are true homophones and cause more problems than most. Write one sentence for each set that includes each of the three words.

1 to two too   2 there their they're

EXTENSION

There is a small group of words that cause confusion, though can easily be understood.

practise practice   advise advice   devise device

The words practise, advise and devise are all verbs, so can have **ing** or **ed** added, whereas practice, advice and device are all nouns, so can not.
For example: We have been **devising** a **device**.
                     verb (action word)   noun (naming word)

A Write a sentence using each of these words.

1 practising   2 practice   3 advised

4 advice   5 devised   6 device

B Some words are spelt differently in American English. Check in your dictionary and write these American words using our normal spelling.

1 defense   2 offense   3 pretense   4 color   5 jewelry   6 theater

7 plow   8 center   9 pajamas   10 woolen   11 flavor   12 harbor

simple plurals

When the **star**s come out the fox**es** run about.

KEY WORDS

stars
plates
horses
clouds
dishes
torches
buses
foxes
babies
cherries
boys
keys

Match a key word to each picture clue.
Underline the letters in each word that make it a plural noun.

1 _____

2 _____

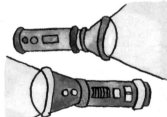

3 _____

4 _____

5 _____

6 _____

7 _____

8 _____

9 _____

Remember, to make a noun **plural** we normally add **s**.
   For example: teacher teacher**s**

But if the noun ends with s, x, ch or sh we add **es**.
   For example:
      bu<u>s</u> bus**es**   fo<u>x</u> fox**es**   chur<u>ch</u> church**es**   bu<u>sh</u> bush**es**

If a noun ends in **y**, we usually change **y** to **i** and add **es**.
   For example: countr<u>y</u> countr**ies**

But if the letter before the **y** is a <u>vowel</u>, simply add **s**.
   For example: d<u>ay</u> day**s**

A Write the plural of each of these words.

1 ash   2 pen   3 glass   4 berry   5 party

6 display 7 penny   8 shoe   9 puppy   10 box

11 key   12 monkey 13 jelly   14 kiss   15 pitch

16 baby   17 tax   18 mother   19 donkey   20 day

B When we make a plural verb singular (e.g. they talk, he talk**s**) we need
to follow the same rules. Write four verbs that follow these rules. One
of each type is done to help you.

+s	+es	+ies
jump jumps	push pushes	hurry hurries

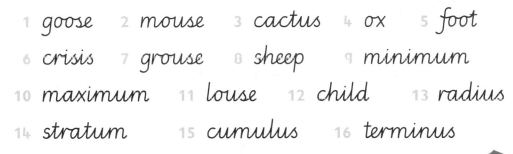

Some nouns don't follow these simple rules. To make some nouns
plural several letters in the word are changed.
   For example: man m**e**n   woman wom**e**n   child child**ren**

Write the plural form of these nouns.

1 goose   2 mouse   3 cactus   4 ox   5 foot

6 crisis   7 grouse   8 sheep   9 minimum

10 maximum   11 louse   12 child   13 radius

14 stratum   15 cumulus   16 terminus

Check your answers in a
dictionary.

more plurals

Where are the hippos hiding?

KEY WORDS

wolves
scarves
loaves
calves
thieves
knives
cliffs
chiefs
volcanoes
potatoes
tomatoes
hippos
cuckoos
cellos

Match a key word to each picture clue.
Underline the letters in each word that make it a plural noun.

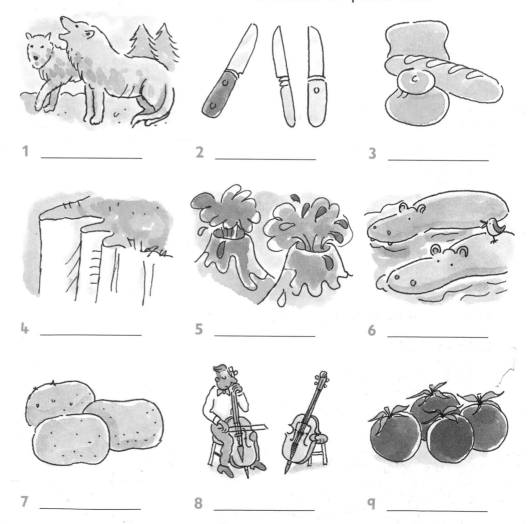

1 _____

2 _____

3 _____

4 _____

5 _____

6 _____

7 _____

8 _____

9 _____

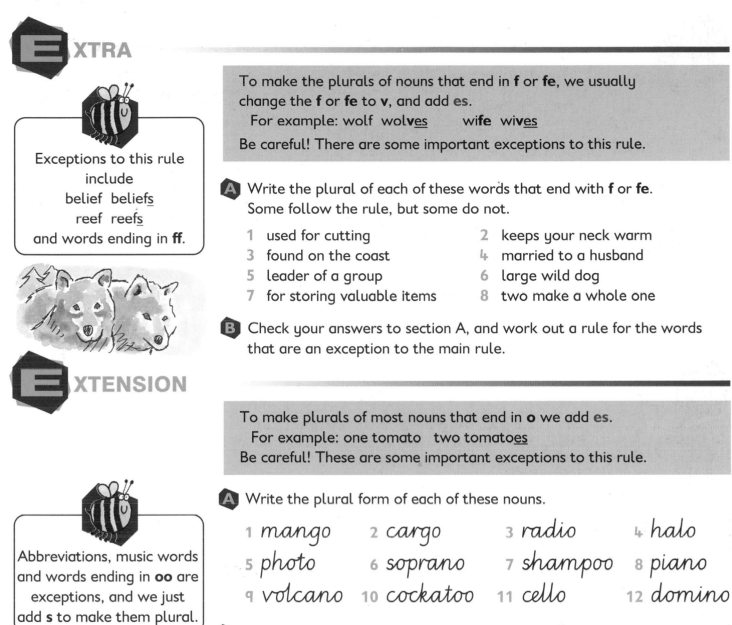

EXTRA

Exceptions to this rule
include
belief beliefs
reef reefs
and words ending in **ff**.

To make the plurals of nouns that end in **f** or **fe**, we usually change the **f** or **fe** to **v**, and add **es**.

For example: wolf wol**ves**   wife wi**ves**

Be careful! There are some important exceptions to this rule.

A Write the plural of each of these words that end with **f** or **fe**. Some follow the rule, but some do not.

1 used for cutting
2 keeps your neck warm
3 found on the coast
4 married to a husband
5 leader of a group
6 large wild dog
7 for storing valuable items
8 two make a whole one

B Check your answers to section A, and work out a rule for the words that are an exception to the main rule.

EXTENSION

To make plurals of most nouns that end in **o** we add **es**.

For example: one tomato   two tomato**es**

Be careful! These are some important exceptions to this rule.

Abbreviations, music words and words ending in **oo** are exceptions, and we just add **s** to make them plural.

A Write the plural form of each of these nouns.

1 mango   2 cargo   3 radio   4 halo
5 photo   6 soprano   7 shampoo   8 piano
9 volcano 10 cockatoo 11 cello   12 domino

B Copy and complete this word puzzle.

clue	number of letters	first letter	plural noun
bouncing sound waves	6	e	
single-horned large African animals (abbreviation)	6	r	
we eat their edible tubers	8	p	
fired from submarines	9	t	
long-legged pink birds	10	f	
large herds used to roam the prairies	9	b	
wild Australian dogs	7	d	

mnemonics

My nan eats mountains of nachos in chilli sauce!

FOCUS

KEY WORDS

teacher
library
reel
bicycle
necessary
separate
chocolate
lightning
twelfth
ambitious
vegetable
parallel
government
weight

A Write a short sentence explaining why each of these pictures can help you to remember how to spell one of the key words.

1 vege<u>table</u>

2 <u>reel</u>

3 <u>tea</u>cher

4 tw<u>elf</u>th

5 w<u>eigh</u>t

6 bi<u>cycle</u>

B Draw a small picture to remind you how to spell a word that you sometimes find difficult.

Remember, **mnemonics** (pronounced 'nemonics') are short phrases or rhymes that help us remember things. We can use mnemonics to help us to remember which homophone to use.

here or hear   We h**ear** with our **ear**s.   It's **here** not t**here**.

A Copy these words and phrases. Underline the letters in each that the mnemonic helps us to remember.

1 knight or night The knight is the king's brother.

2 stake or steak   I leant the rake against the stake.

3 cellar or seller The cellar is like a prison cell.

4 bear or bare   The bear bit my ear.

B Make up your own mnemonics to help you remember which of these homophones to use.

1 grown or groan   2 fair or fare   3 check or cheque   4 pail or pale

EXTENSION

A Copy the mnemonics below. In each one underline the letters in each word that the mnemonic helps us to remember. Use the mnemonics to learn how to spell the six words.

1 separate — Rats never forget how to spell separate.

2 parallel — Parallel has two parallel lines in the middle.

3 device, advice, practice — Ice is a noun as are device, advice and practice.

4 dictionary — Mary's dictionary won't help her diction.

5 government — Our government governs us.

6 necessary — Be careful of the cess pool in the middle of necessary!

B Create mnemonics for these tricky words, or choose some other words that you particularly want to learn.

1 lightning   2 chocolate   3 friend   4 innocent   5 island

prefixes

FOCUS

KEY WORDS

disappointed
dissatisfied
dissimilar

unsure
unnecessary
unnatural

overseas
overrule
overreact

impatient
immobile
immovable

The rule when adding a prefix is: 'Just add it!'
Don't change or miss out any letters.
  For example: un + sure = unsure

Sometimes, adding a prefix creates a double letter.
  For example: dis + satisfy = di<u>ss</u>atisfy

The double **s** is caused by bringing together the last letter of the prefix with the first letter of the word. Don't be tempted to leave out an **s**.

A Add these prefixes to their roots, being careful to remember the rule.

1 dis	+	satisfy	service	jointed
		able	similar	solve
2 un	+	necessary	occupied	nerve
		numbered	natural	named
3 over	+	react	seas	rule
		ride	rated	run
4 im	+	possible	migrate	mortal
		modest	mature	movable

B Write a word that uses each of these prefixes, and whose root begins with the same letter as the last letter of the prefix. Use each word in your own sentence, to show what it means. You will find a dictionary helpful for this exercise.

  1 mis   2 inter   3 pre   4 re

EXTRA

Many prefixes used in English originally came from other languages, but some are English words and are therefore easier to spell.
  For example, 'down' is a prefix in:
  downbeat downcast downfall downhill downpour downtrodden
Sometimes we need to use a hyphen when adding a suffix.
  For example, over-hasty over-confident over-protective

There are more than a hundred **over** words!

A Write three words that begin with each of these prefixes.

1 out   2 under   3 super   4 up   5 be

B There are a large number of words that have the prefix **over**.
How many can you think of? Write them in your book.

C Copy these groups of words. Neatly underline the prefix in each word.
Use a dictionary to find the meaning of each of the words.
Write what you think the prefix means.

1 microchip   microfilm   microscope
2 forecast   foretell   foresee
3 antiseptic   antibiotic   antifreeze   antidote
4 submarine   subway   subsonic
5 precaution   prepare   preface

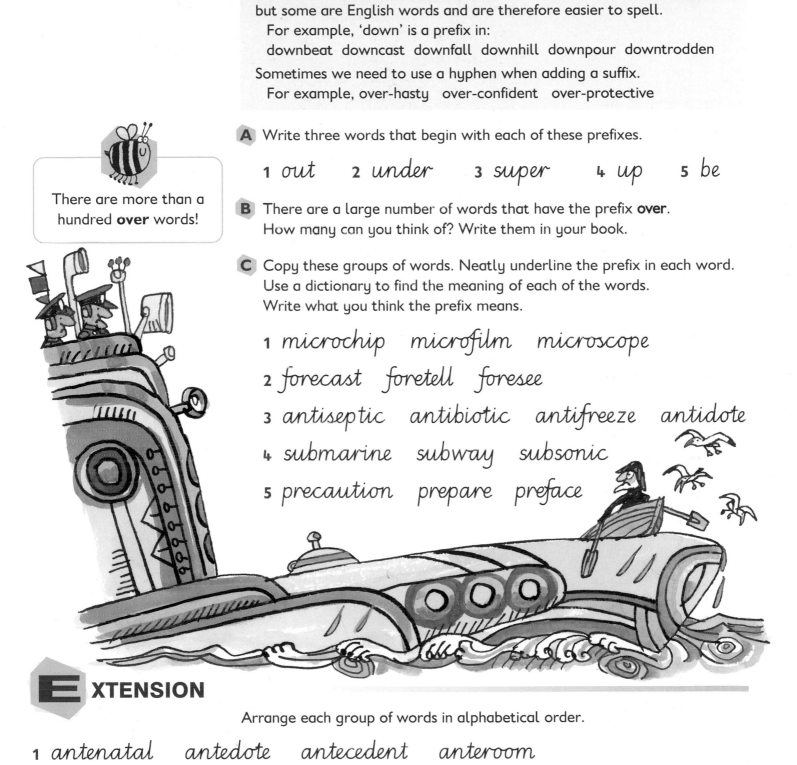

EXTENSION

Arrange each group of words in alphabetical order.

1 antenatal   antedote   antecedent   anteroom
2 contrary   contraflow   contradiction   contravene   contralto
3 discharge   disappear   disagreement   disappointing   dissatisfied
4 international   interface   interval   intervene   interjection

suffixes

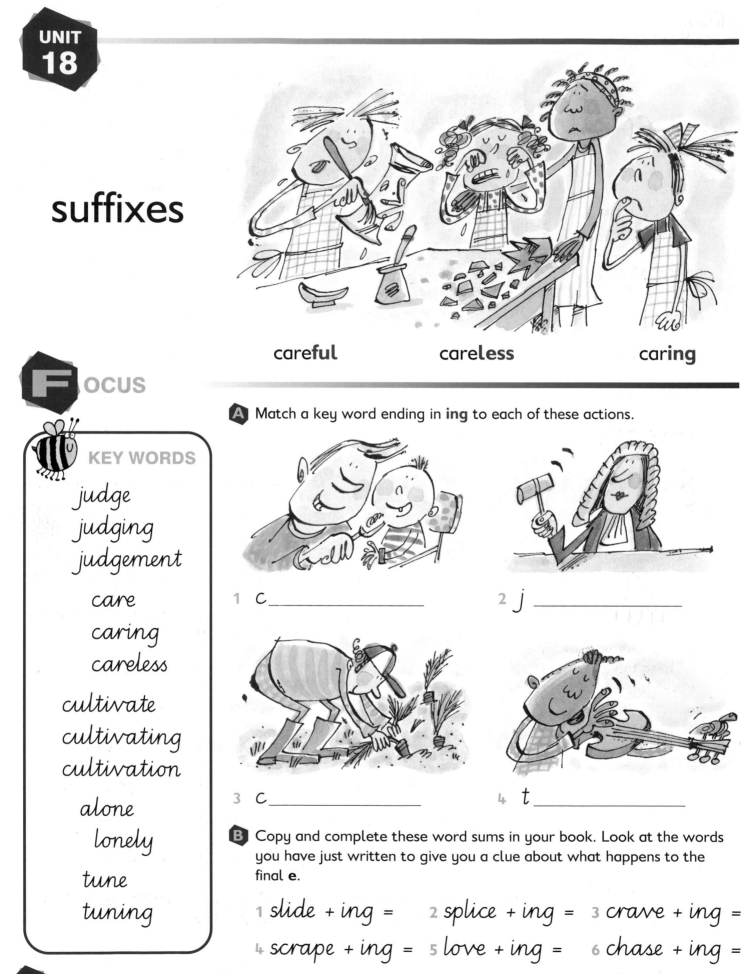

careful   **careless**   **caring**

FOCUS

KEY WORDS

judge
judging
judgement
care
caring
careless
cultivate
cultivating
cultivation
alone
lonely
tune
tuning

A Match a key word ending in **ing** to each of these actions.

1 c_____

2 j _____

3 c_____

4 t _____

B Copy and complete these word sums in your book. Look at the words you have just written to give you a clue about what happens to the final **e**.

1 slide + ing =   2 splice + ing =   3 crave + ing =

4 scrape + ing =   5 love + ing =   6 chase + ing =

EXTRA

Suffixes beginning with vowels are called **vowel suffixes** and those beginning with consonants are **consonant suffixes**.

To add a suffix when a word ends with **e**
- drop the **e** if the suffix begins with a **vowel**
  For example: wak<u>e</u> + **ing** = waking   sham<u>e</u> + **ed** = shamed
- keep the **e** if the suffix begins with a **consonant**
  For example: wak<u>e</u> + **ful** = wakeful   shame + **less** = shameless

Some exceptions to this rule include:
    true truly   argue argument   due duly

Add these suffixes to each of the words. Write the new word that is formed.

1 package + ing =

2 place + ed =

3 manage + ment =

4 safe + ty =

5 combine + ation =

6 judge + ment =

7 relate + ion =

8 argue + ing =

9 imagine + ation =

10 share + ing =

11 care + less =

12 insure + ance =

EXTENSION

When adding the vowel suffixes **able** or **ible** to a word that ends with **e**, we nearly always first drop the **e**. But there are some important exceptions!

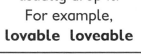

Americans sometimes keep the **e** where we would usually drop it. For example, **lovable loveable**

A Complete these word sums. Use your dictionary to spot the four words in this group that must keep their final **e** when the suffix is added.

1 value + able =

2 change + able =

3 cure + able =

4 peace + able =

5 believe + able =

6 recognise + able =

7 sense + ible =

8 notice + able =

9 desire + able =

10 response + ible =

11 love + able =

12 service + able =

B Work out and write down a rule to help you remember which words keep their final **e** when the vowel suffix is added.

more suffixes

funny

funn**ily**

funn**ier**

FOCUS

KEY WORDS

marry
married
marriage

funny
funnily
funnier

geology
geological

melody
melodious

bounty
bountiful

skill
skilful

A Copy each of these verbs into your book. Next to each write the word with **ed** added. Remember to change the **y** to **i**.

1 *worry*

2 *carry*

3 *bury*

4 *marry*

5 *hurry*

6 *mutiny*

B Write three more words ending in **y** which follow the same rule.

 **EXTRA**

> To add a suffix to a word that ends in **y** (where the **y** sounds like the i in tin), change the **y** to an **i** and add the suffix.
>   For example: ugl**y**   ugl**i**ness

A Add these suffixes to these words.

1 merry + ment   2 marry + age   3 crazy + est   4 funny + ly

5 naughty + ness   6 stormy + er   7 happy + ly   8 geology + cal

9 jolly + ty   10 necessary + ly   11 subsidy + sed   12 energy + sed

13 duty + ful   14 botany + cal   15 choosy + est   16 beauty + fully

17 happy + ness   18 gloomy + est   19 bounty + ful   20 melody + ous

B Find and write six other examples of where **y** at the end of a word has been change to **i** when the suffix has been added.

 **EXTENSION**

> To add a suffix ending with **ll** to many words, we drop one **l**.
>   For example: doubt + fu**ll** = doubtful
>
> If the word also ends with **ll**, we sometimes delete one **l** from the word, as well as one from the suffix.
>   For example: wi**ll** + fu**ll** = wilful
>
> However, this is not a 'rule' as there are several exceptions, especially words with a **ness** suffix.
>   For example: stillness

A Join these together. Check your answers in a dictionary. Some are exceptions to the rule.

1 skill + full   2 thought + full   3 full + fill

4 full + ness   5 joy + full   6 fate + full

7 shrill + ness   8 hill + side   9 care + full

B Look in your dictionary and list the words that begin with the sound **all** (as in b**all**), such as **al**mighty.
Write a rule about what you notice.

CHECK-UP 2

OCUS

Write the word that each of these pictures reminds you of.
One letter is given to help you.

1 g_____

2 _r_____

3 t_____

4 c_____

5 w_____

6 c_____

7 d_____

8 _n_____

9 l_____

10 c_____

11 s_____

12 m_____

A One letter has been omitted from each word. Write them correctly in your book.

1 paral_se   2 catastroph_   3 archa_ology

4 _sychology   5 g_ography   6 autobiogra_hy

B Write the correct spelling of each of these frequently misspelt mathematical words.

1 curcumfrence   2 parralel   3 centimeter

4 approximatly   5 horizontle   6 symetrical

C Write a homophone for each of these words.

1 brake   2 site   3 aloud   4 piece   5 sauce   6 there

D Write the plural form of these words.

1 ash   2 box   3 jelly   4 woman

5 louse   6 cactus   7 calf   8 cliff

9 volcano   10 piano   11 cuckoo   12 belief

E Write a word that begins with each of these prefixes.

1 micro   2 anti   3 fore

F Add these suffixes to these words.

1 package + ing   2 marry + age   3 combine + ation   4 funny + ly

5 insure + ance   6 necessary + ly   7 subsidy + sed   8 relate + ion

EXTENSION

A Write the noun to which each of these verbs is related.

1 practising   2 licensing   3 advised   4 devising

B Write a mnemonic to help you remember how to spell these words.

1 interrupt   2 imaginary   3 concentration

C Arrange these words in alphabetical order.

intrepid   intransitive   intrigue

intricate   intravenous

D Join these roots and suffixes.

1 skill + full   2 joy + full   3 full + fill   4 fate + full

ie
ei

Eight fri**e**nds in a f**ie**ld!

F OCUS

KEY WORDS

belief
hygiene
believe
field
friend
patient
review
receive
perceive
either
protein
freight
rein
forfeit

It is helpful to remember that **i** comes before **e** when the sound is **ee**.
  For example: rel**ie**ve, pr**ie**st

But **i** does **not** come before **e** when following a **c**.
  For example: dec**ei**ve, rec**ei**pt

And **i** does **not** come before **e** when the sound is not **ee**.
  For example: h**ei**r, for**ei**gn

1 Write the words in the box below in a long list.

> receive field believe wield weigh eight
> their deceit rein chief shield vein
> receipt sleight leisure achieve

2 Tick the words in which the **ie** or the **ei** sounds **ee** (as in b**ee**).

3 Underline those you have ticked that have an **ei**.

EXTRA

Whilst it is helpful to remember the little rhyme –
  i before **e**, except after **c**,
– there are some exceptions.

A There are seven different sounds made by **ie** or **ei**.
Copy this chart and use it to group the key words according to the
sound made by **ie** or **ei**. The first two words have been done to help you.

ie or ei sounds like	ie words	ei words
ee as in cr<u>ee</u>k	diesel	seize
ay as in w<u>ay</u>		
i as in b<u>i</u>t		
y as in m<u>y</u>		
e as in b<u>e</u>st		
u as in h<u>u</u>nt		
oo as in b<u>oo</u>t		

B Add some more **ie** or **ei** words to your groups.

EXTENSION

In all the examples in the chart above, the two letters **ie** and **ei** form a
single sound or digraph. But there are other words where the two
letters are pronounced separately.
  For example: cri<u>er</u>   d<u>ei</u>ty

A Copy each of these words into your book, completing the gap
with **ie** or **ei**.

1 cloth _ r   2 r _ nforce   3 spontan _ ity

4 cop _ r   5 obed _ nce   6 sc _ nce

7 r _ terate   8 med _ val   9 homogen _ ty

B Check your answers to A in your dictionary.

history and geography words

castle · cathedral · settlement · country

KEY WORDS

castle
cathedral
parliament
government
document
revolution
longitude
latitude
location
settlement
county
country

Look at these pictures. Select and write a key word that matches each one.

1 _____

2 _____

3 _____

4 _____

5 _____

6 _____

7 _____

8 _____

EXTRA

All of these history words are misspelt in a way that often happens. Write them correctly.

When you have finished check your answers in a dictionary.

1 independance 2 defense 3 citizon

4 parlament 5 govenment 6 emmegration

7 riegn 8 religon 9 republick

10 revolushun 11 seige 12 traiter

EXTENSION

A Match a word from the box to each of these definitions.

volcano	atlas	estuary	longitude
contour	settlement	landscape	erosion

1 a book of maps
2 a line on a map marking points of equal height
3 a gradual wearing away
4 the mouth of a river, where it enters the sea
5 a wide view of the countryside
6 a mountain formed by molten rock emerging from deep in the earth
7 a place where people decide to live close together
8 the distance of a place east or west of Greenwich

B Copy each of these words in turn, writing next to each a simple definition. Use a dictionary to help you.

1 latitude 2 urban 3 amenity

4 climate 5 constitution 6 colony

7 propaganda 8 immigration 9 emmigration

ent ence
ant ance

Silent eleph**ant**
Obedient eleph**ant**
Intelligent eleph**ant**
Distant eleph**ant**

FOCUS

KEY WORDS

silent
silence
evident
evidence
violent
violence
different
difference
distant
distance
important
importance
assistant
assistance

A Copy these sentences into your book.
Add the missing endings.

1 There was no noise, it was totally sil_____.

2 The police said they could find no evid_____.

3 This argument won't be settled by viol_____.

4 We will be going to a differ_____ school next year.

5 The shop assist_____ was very helpful.

6 Her discovery was of great import_____.

B Write your own sentence using **innocent** and **innocence**.

EXTRA

A Match these adjectives with their nouns.
Write them in pairs in your book.

adjectives	nouns
distant	assistance
silent	elegance
innocent	ignorance
obedient	intelligence
ignorant	obedience
intelligent	innocence
elegant	silence
assistant	distance

B Make a noun from each of these adjectives. Write them in your book.

1 important   2 fragrant   3 absent   4 evident

5 convenient 6 violent   7 abundant   8 different

EXTENSION

Adverbs describe actions.
Many adverbs are made by adding **ly** to a noun, like this:
efficient + **ly** = efficient**ly**

A Copy these into your book.

1 effici____   2 sil____   3 import____   4 frequ____

5 abund____   6 viol____   7 intellig____   8 innoc____

Remember,
an **adverb** usually
describes a verb.

B 1 Add **ent** or **ant** to each one to make an adjective.
2 Make an adverb from each adjective.
3 Write a phrase or short sentence to use each adverb you have made.
The first one is done to help you.

1 efficient   efficiently
   He worked efficiently and had soon finished.

unstressed letters

KEY WORDS

family
boundary
raspberry
postpone
doctor
listener
different
separate
desperate
factory
dustbin
generally
generous
interesting

A Copy the word grid below. Write the answers to the clues in the correct rows of the grid.

1 not the same

2 to put off until later

3 a place where things are made

4 container for rubbish

5 the outer edge of a cricket field

6 a soft red berry

1									

If your answers are all correct, the letters in the shaded box will make another key word.

B The answer to each of these clues has a letter that is either unsounded when the word is read aloud, or is not sounded very distinctly. Circle the letters that are unstressed.

EXTRA

Here are some more spellings with **unstressed vowels**. Remember, unstressed vowels are vowel letters which are difficult to make out because they are spoken quickly, or are sounded very quietly.

Some words have **unstressed consonants**.

dus̲tbin is often pronounced *dusbin*

i̲ron   is often pronounced *ion*

A Copy these words. Circle the unstressed vowels or consonants and write a mnemonic for four of the trickier words to help you remember how to spell them in future.

1 shepherd   2 voluntary   3 cupboard
4 parliament   5 medicine   6 postpone
7 poisonous   8 interested   9 jewellery
10 literacy   11 miniature   12 geography

Remember, a **mnemonic** is a phrase or rhyme to help you remember a spelling.

B Write the two homophones **stationary** and **stationery** in your book. Next to each write a sentence to show what the word means. The mnemonic 'buy stationery from a stationer' might help you.

EXTENSION

It can sometimes help to spell words correctly that have unstressed vowels if we think of the syllables.

Remember, every syllable needs a vowel.

separate   se / pa / rate

This reminds us not to spell the word *seprate*.

A Copy each of these words into your book, saying them aloud as you do. Next to each word write its syllables. The first one is done to help you.

1 frightening frigh / ten / ing   2 business
3 prosperous   4 miniature   5 compromise
6 company 7 voluntary 8 abandoned 9 generous

B Use a dictionary to help you spot the unstressed vowels that have been left out of these words. Write them correctly in your book.

1 desprate   2 primry   3 misrable
4 refrence   5 intresting 6 marvllous
7 orignal   8 easly   9 hospitl

more tricky words

I would if I could but **I can't**.
I know that you **wouldn't** so I **won't**.

FOCUS

KEY WORDS

I'm
we're
isn't
can't
won't
beginning
interrupt
disappointed
argument
audience
evidence
research
conscience
sequence

I'm I'll I've I'd we'll we've we're
isn't weren't wasn't wouldn't won't can't
it's what's where's who's who'll

A Match a contraction from the box with these pairs of words.
Write them in your book. The first one is done to help you.

1 I am = I'm 2 is not = 3 who is = 4 what is =

5 I would = 6 we are = 7 will not = 8 where is =

9 we will = 10 it is = 11 I will = 12 who will =

B What are these contractions short for?

1 I'm = 2 I'll = 3 I've = 4 I'd =

5 we'll = 6 we're = 7 isn't = 8 weren't =

9 wouldn't = 10 won't = 11 can't = 12 what's =

EXTRA

In each of these words one of the letters should have been doubled. Write the words correctly into your book.

1 accomodation 2 asessment 3 begining

4 disapeared 5 disapoint 6 embarass

7 hapened 8 interupt 9 mariage

10 necesary 11 patern 12 posession

13 questionaire 14 sucess 15 symetrical

16 tomorow

EXTENSION

Here are some more frequently misspelt words. Write them correctly, using a dictionary to help you where necessary.

1 arguement 2 audince 3 beleave

4 beried 5 colume 6 consence

7 creaton 8 evidense 9 fourty

10 helthy 11 lovley 12 jelous

13 mischeif 14 potental 15 reserch

16 secondry

ICT words

monitor

www.nelsonthornes.com

Internet

computer

keyboard

KEY WORDS

cable
CD-ROM
computer
disk
electronic
hardware
Internet
keyboard
memory
monitor
mouse
program
spreadsheet
software
virus

A Look at these small pictures. Select and write a key word that matches each one.

1 _____   2 _____   3 _____   4 _____

5 _____   6 _____   7 _____   8 _____

www.nelson thornes.com

B List the key words that are not illustrated in A. Next to each, write a brief definition. Use your dictionary for help.

All of these computing words are misspelt in a way that often happens. Write them correctly.

When you have finished check your answers in a dictionary.

1	programme	2	ikon	3	processer
4	megabite	5	curser	6	disc
7	grafics	8	multymedia	9	daterbase
10	parsword	11	virrus	12	moniter

EXTENSION

Netspeak
is the language of the Internet.

A The Internet has its own language and if you want to surf in style, you'll need to understand it.
Copy these words and next to each write what it means.

1	email	2	browser	3	cyberspace
4	domain	5	keypals	6	logon
7	newbie	8	nick	9	signature

B Spelling is notoriously bad on the Internet. Sometimes this is due to typing errors but often it is deliberate.
For example, numbers may be used for letters, such as
8 for **ate**, as in **C U L8R** (*see you later*).

Make up some spellings yourself using numbers in place of some letters.

British English or American English

My **favourite flavour**   My **favorite flavor**

FOCUS

KEY WORDS

centre
center
flavour
flavor
defence
defense
travelled
traveled
organise
organize
programme
program

A Use the words in the key word box to help you work out how these American words are spelt in Britain. Write the answers in your book.

1 fiber   2 theater   3 flavor   4 harbor

5 offense   6 leveling   7 program   8 canceled

B Write a sentence about what you have noticed about the difference between the way Americans and British people spell these words.

Tuesday's performance is Cancelled

EXIT

Many of the words where American spelling is different from British spelling were originally French words. Usually, we have kept the French spellings whilst the Americans have changed the spellings slightly.

For example: favour   favor

Be very careful with these – they do unexpected things!

A We have kept the **our** in some French-derived words where the Americans use **or**. Write in your book **British** or **American** for each of these words.

1 harbour	2 labor	3 humor	4 flavour
5 favorite	6 harboring	7 parlour	8 flavoring

B We are not always consistent when spelling words. Join together these root words and suffixes, but check your answers in a dictionary. Write a sentence to explain what you notice.

1 humour + ous   2 honour + able   3 discolour + ation

4 vigour + ous   5 vapour + ise   6 honour + ary

7 colour + ing   8 invigour + ate   9 humour + ist

EXTENSION

Copy these sentences, changing any American spellings to the British versions, as we would write them.

1 We went to the theater and first saw an incredibly humorous comedian with a gray, curly mustache.

2 We all thought his act was marvelous.

3 Second on the program was an aging pop star, dripping in cheap jewelry, who said she had traveled from New York to sing.

4 Dad said he thought her voice was dreadful and her dress didn't look as good as his old, colored pajamas!

5 "I hope they improve the caliber of their performers or I'm in favor of canceling the tickets we have bought for next month," he added.

6 "Where's your sense of humor gone?" joked Mum.

OCUS

Write the word that goes with each of these pictures.
One letter is given to help you.

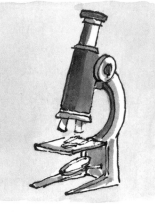

1 t_____ 2 d_____ 3 m_____ 4 b_____

5 b_____ 6 b_____ 7 t_____ 8 c_____f__

9 l_____ 10 f_____ 11 e_____ 12 c_____

A Copy and complete these word wheels in your book.

appoint

happy

B Write the small words that make up these connectives.

1 meanwhile   2 therefore   3 insomuch   4 notwithstanding

C The unstressed vowels are omitted from these words. Write them in your book correctly.

1 desprate   2 busness   3 diffrently   4 genrally
5 litrature   6 religon   7 parliment   8 necessry

D Write the correct spelling of each of these frequently misspelt science words.

1 evaperation   2 condensashun   3 resparation
4 apratus   5 thermometre   6 labroratry

E Write a homophone for each of these words.

1 beach   2 key   3 stair   4 vane   5 feet   6 ewe

F Write the plural form of these words.

1 bush   2 fox   3 cherry   4 child   5 mouse   6 radius
7 wolf   8 cliff   9 tomato   10 cello   11 shampoo   12 chief

G Write a word that begins with each of these prefixes.

1 inter   2 ante   3 over

H Write the adjectives to which each of these nouns is related.

1 distance   2 silence   3 intelligence   4 elegance

I Join together these root words and suffixes, but check your answers in a dictionary.
Write a sentence to explain what you notice.

1 vigour + ous   2 honour + ary   3 vapour + ise
4 invigour + ate   5 humour + ist

A Write two words that have each of these Greek or Latin roots.

1 *liber* (free) 2 *dec* (ten) 3 *audi* (to hear) 4 *mono* (single)

B What are the syllables in each of these words?

1 microphone   2 pedestrian

3 centipede   4 geographical

C What are the 'guide words' in your dictionary on the page in which these words are listed?

1 autograph   2 navigation   3 export   4 suspect

D Add **ent** or **ant** to each one to make an adjective.

1 abs_____   2 dist_____   3 evid_____   4 ignor_____

E Write a mnemonic to help you remember how to spell these words.

1 island   2 manufacture

3 centipede   4 proportion

F Arrange these words in alphabetical order.

obstruct obtuse obtain obstruction obsolete